Blogging
for Educators

Blogging
for Educators
Writing for Professional Learning

Starr Sackstein

A SAGE Company

FOR INFORMATION:

Corwin

A SAGE Company

2455 Teller Road

Thousand Oaks, California 91320

(800) 233-9936

www.corwin.com

SAGE Publications Ltd.

1 Oliver's Yard

55 City Road

London EC1Y 1SP

United Kingdom

SAGE Publications India Pvt. Ltd.

B 1/I 1 Mohan Cooperative Industrial Area

Mathura Road, New Delhi 110 044

India

SAGE Publications Asia-Pacific Pte. Ltd.

3 Church Street

#10-04 Samsung Hub

Singapore 049483

Printed in the United States of America

A catalog record of this book is available from the Library of Congress.

ISBN 978-1-4833-7779-7

This book is printed on acid-free paper.

Executive Editor: Arnis Burvikovs

Associate Editor: Ariel Price

Editorial Assistant: Andrew Olson

Production Editor: Amy Schroller

Copy Editor: Tammy Giesmann

Typesetter: C&M Digitals (P) Ltd.

Proofreader: Laura Webb

Cover and Interior Design: Janet Kiesel

Marketing Manager: Lisa Lysne

SUSTAINABLE FORESTRY INITIATIVE

Certified Chain of Custody
Promoting Sustainable Forestry
www.sfiprogram.org
SFI-01268

SFI label applies to text stock

15 16 17 18 19 10 9 8 7 6 5 4 3 2 1

Contents

Preface

Welcome to the Corwin Connected Educators Series.

Last year, Ariel Price, Arnis Burvikovs, and I assembled a great list of authors for the Fall 2014 books in the Corwin Connected Educators Series. As leaders in their field of connected education, they all provided practical, short books that helped educators around the world find new ways to connect. The books in the Spring 2015 season will be equally as beneficial for educators.

We have all seen momentous changes for educators. States debate the use of the Common Core State Standards, and teachers and leaders still question the use of technology, while some of their students have to disconnect and leave it at home because educators do not know how to control learning on devices. Many of the Series authors worked in schools where they were sometimes the only ones trying to encourage use of technology tools at the same time their colleagues tried to ban it. Through their PLNs they were able to find others who were trying to push the envelope.

This spring, we have a list of authors who are known for pushing the envelope. Some are people who wrote books for the Fall 2014 season, while others are brand new to the series. What they have in common is that they see a different type of school for students, and they write about ideas that all schools should be practicing now.

Rafranz Davis discusses *The Missing Voices in EdTech*. She looks at and discusses how we need to bring more diverse voices to the connected world because those voices will enrich how we learn and the way we think. Starr Sackstein, a teacher in New York City writes about blogging for reflection in her book *Blogging for Educators*. Twitter powerhouse Steven W. Anderson returns to the Series to bring us *Content Curation*, as do the very engaging Joseph M. Sanfelippo and Tony Sinanis with their new book, *Principal Professional Development*. Mark Barnes rounds out the comeback authors with his book on *5 Skills for the Global Learner*. Thomas C. Murray and Jeffrey Zoul bring a very practical "how to" for teachers and leaders in their book *Leading Professional Learning*, and Makerspaces extraordinaire Laura Fleming brings her expertise with *Worlds of Making*.

I am insanely excited about this book series. As a former principal I know time is in short supply, and teachers and leaders need something they can read today and put into practice tomorrow. That is the exciting piece about technology; it can help enhance your practices by providing you with new ideas and helping you connect with educators around the world.

The books can be read in any order, and each will provide information on the tools that will keep us current in the digital age. We also look forward to continuing the series with more books from experts on connectedness.

As Michael Fullan has been saying for many years, technology is not the right driver, good pedagogy is, and the books in this connected series focus on practices that will lead to good pedagogy in our digital age. To assist readers in their connected experience, we have created the Corwin Connected Educators companion website where readers can connect with the authors and find resources to help further their experience. The website can be found at www.corwin.com/connectededucators. It is our hope that we can meet you where you are in your digital journey, and bring you up to the next level.

Peter DeWitt, EdD @PeterMDeWitt

About the Author

 **Starr Sackstein** currently works at World Journalism Preparatory School in Flushing, NY, as a high school English and Journalism teacher and is the author of *Teaching Mythology Exposed: Helping Teachers Create Visionary Classroom Perspective*. This year she began a new blog with *Education Week Teacher* called "Work in Progress" in addition to her personal blog StarrSackstein.com where she discusses all aspects of being a teacher. Sackstein co-moderates #jerdchat and #sunchat as well as contributes to #NYedChat. This year she has made the Bammy Awards finals for Secondary High School Educator. In speaking engagements, Sackstein speaks about blogging, journalism education and bring your own device (BYOD), helping people see technology doesn't have to be feared.

*Thank you to my parents who have always encouraged me
to write because it has always been my first love, even when I was going to school
for medicine, and to my students who continue to teach me to grow as a person and
provide so much for me to reflect on while I write; this one's for you.*

*Mostly, thanks to my son who reminds me
always to see the world through the eyes of a child.*

Introduction

B logging is an important tool for education leaders and students. Since writing is a vital part of communication, blogging brings those essential skills to virtual connection; it takes the 140 characters of Twitter and develops the sound byte into reflective depth for formative learning. Generating an online space to openly share ideas and reflections richens the complete educational experience.

Unfortunately, not every educator is prepared with the necessary twenty-first century skills to blog regularly or teach kids how to develop an online presence. Learning what a blog is and how and why educators need to be doing it, teachers and administrators will have a better understanding of how to start a blog quickly and turn small bits of writing time into a tool for growth. They are then able to turn that knowledge into an effective teaching tool for their students.

With the Common Core Standards and other state standards being a part of the changing educational landscape, reflection has been brought into the forefront of our collective consciousness. Although many of us believed it before, we now are actually discussing and implementing new reflective tools to help students and educators develop more metacognitive skills; it is in this way we learn to foster an authentic voice with a deeper understanding of our strengths and challenges. Blogging is a space to do this—but not just within the confines of a journal with an audience who wants to connect and participate in that growth.

The development of an audience increases the level of urgency we place upon ourselves to commit to the act of writing. When others are waiting to hear what we have to say or waiting for us to provide feedback on what they've said, we generate a reciprocal relationship that strengthens each person in a number of different ways: it strengthens our ability to be honest about who we are and what we want, it allows us to see ourselves as others see us and how that contrasts with what we feel inside, it provides a realistic sounding board for challenges we face individually that don't have to be faced alone, and it offers us an opportunity to brand ourselves in an authentic way to promote a community of learning.

Before each of us has become inhibited by the rules of society and the learned behaviors of others, we see the world with curiosity and life, nothing is impossible. As we grow, we still know this within, but allow outside factors to separate us from this core belief. Blogging is one way to get back in touch with ourselves and communicate the truth of our experiences with others.

Throughout this book, the reader will take away many things, most importantly a practical approach to developing a blogging routine and an inroad to teaching students to do the same thing. When leaders in an educational community can speak from genuine experience and encourage others to take that initial leap, they become better equipped to support those around them to grow as people, in turn making the community stronger.

Learning Intentions:

By the end of this book you will know:

- What blogging is and why educators should do it
- How to blog and which platform to do it on
- Who we blog for
- How to use blogging to connect

Why Blog?

Remember when we used to write in journals? They were of various kinds—large notebooks with lines or without, decorated covers, full of color and memories. Visceral joy and importance is what I felt when I was given a pretty pink diary with a lock—a place to keep my darkest eight-year-old secrets and dreams. Although small, it held the hope of possibilities to come. Taking pen to paper daily, I wrote about everything. It all seemed important back then, but more essential than *what* I wrote was the habit I developed for writing regularly. This practice has grown with me into adulthood, and because of it, I'm able to develop as a person, educator, and writer every day. That diary was the beginning of a lifelong dream to write and of the belief in myself that I could.

> If you want to truly be a writer, you need an audience.

Unfortunately, extended writing is not a regular practice for most people. So many of us are pulled in multiple directions, which makes it impossible for us to make time to think and reflect about what we do and how we can do it better. Blogging is a way to do that and connect with others while we do; it deserves to be made a part of our regular pedagogical routine, if not our life diet as well. That pink diary was definitely special, but it was lonely, and on some level, I knew, even back then that if I wanted to truly be a writer, an audience was necessary. The safety of knowing that the lock on the diary kept my words hostage allowed me to fear no ideas. Only my own judgment could plague me, so I never worried about what others thought. Although blogging is personal, it's also public; therefore, we need to write through our fears and insecurities, humbling ourselves into honest meditation on matters of importance. It may be difficult at first to be completely honest given the transparency, but the more we are able to look within without prejudice, the greater truth we will find in our reflections.

The Fear of Sounding Stupid (A sample post)

"I can't write!"

"No one wants to read what I have to say."

"Why does this even matter, I keep a journal and no one checks my spelling?"

Excuses! We are full of them. If it isn't one thing, it's something else, but the simple fact of the matter is when we don't want to do something, the dissenting voices grow louder.

Isn't that true?

Think about the last time you decided you'd start an exercise regime or a new diet, maybe you were going to read more or try to balance work and life . . .

Blogging is just like any of that, important but easily dismissed for more comfortable or less taxing activities.

As human beings, most of us naturally reflect on decisions we make or share in conversations about the events of our days. Blogging is a way to extend those thoughts or conversations to the page; the posts becoming a log or record to grow by, an opportunity to assess our decisions and consider the impact with hindsight.

As children, some of us marked our growth on door jambs, eagerly watching the progress up the wall, each inch a milestone or coming of age. Blogging can act much the same way for our emotional and intellectual growth.

But why should I blog, you might ask? Keeping a journal is private and acts much the same way, right?

Not really.

By opening your thoughts, challenges, growth, reflection, or celebrations up to an audience, you add a collaborative element that can really change who you are as an educator and a person. A shared experience is far more powerful than one that will never be returned to. Let's face it, how many of us actually go back and read through old journals regularly, then reflect? The journal acts more as a dumping ground rather than a progressive, living document.

Here Are Some Reasons to Blog:

- When you have an audience, you are more accountable to experiences and yourself, there's no room for adjusting reality or denying it.
- Writing routinely will enhance your abilities as a writer and develop increased writing and thinking stamina.
- It will develop your unique teaching voice.
- It will provide opportunities for reflection on all aspects of the teaching experience.

(Continued)

(Continued)

- People will read and share their ideas, which may help solve a problem you've had in a way you wouldn't have thought of given the collaborative experience. Shared ideas are stronger with the collective experience of others.
- You will garner support from strangers in rough times, who will grow to be friends through a shared experience.
- Sharing our journey helps other readers whether they comment or not. Education is a challenging field to work in, and the more support we have the better for everyone.
- You will never need to feel alone again because someone else has been there; I guarantee it.
- You can be a creator of published content.

Still Feeling Skeptical?

When I started blogging a little less than two years ago, I got excited if a handful of people read my blog each day. I used to check my Google analytics obsessively. (Actually I had my friend check them for me because I was intimidated by the dashboard and felt ill-equipped to do it by myself.)

My posts weren't much at first, actually kind of subpar, maybe just a presentation from a conference or a picture with a caption. My earliest posts are slightly embarrassing now, but I had to start somewhere, and since that day, my posts have become more honest and insightful as I've grown braver about sharing with the support of my personal learning network (PLN).

So if you are still wondering why or when you should start, there's no time like the present! Posts don't need to be long only thoughtful. Don't even worry about mistakes at first, just write (that's advice I give the kids).

What is keeping you or had kept you from blogging? Please share

The Impetus to Start

"This blogging thing just isn't for me." I'd be lying if I said that I didn't think this before I started blogging. As a matter of fact, a friend of mine set up my blog, got me a personalized URL and hosted site, and offered to help me start, but I was still resistant. At first he did all the posting for me. Honestly, I still didn't understand the value. Still isolated in my small teaching world, largely unconnected at that point, I refused to take my blinders off. Being comfortable was more important than taking risks, and although I believed I was good, I didn't see a need to do more than I was doing.

There were many excuses I made for not starting my blog, but it was never that I didn't want to write. I just didn't think anyone else was interested in what I had to say.

IT STARTED WITH TWITTER

One day at school we had a guest speaker. Alan November from November Learning talked at a professional development event about technology in education. He introduced us to Twitter. Seemed cool . . . so cool, I signed up on the spot. And then did nothing with it afterward. Like many of my colleagues in the room that day, signing up seemed appropriate while someone else was walking us through it. I wasn't the only one who took the plunge, but with only a couple of exceptions, I'm the only one who eventually unburied Twitter and made it a part of my everyday life.

It took me approximately another year before I started using the social networking site regularly, and now I can't imagine it not being a part of my educational routine. This is what happened with my blogging too. It wasn't for a lack of encouragement: the person who was maintaining my blog for me insisted it was easy and that it had many benefits that would help me get to the next place in my career. At that point, I wasn't ready. Readiness has a lot to do with integrating change into a seemingly functioning routine. It takes guts and bravery.

At first, I didn't understand Twitter or its value, but once I did, I recognized the power of microblogging—140 characters to express ideas and communicate with others quickly, in real time. After lurking on Twitter for a little bit, I saw that people often shared their blog posts, which I read regularly, but still didn't feel like what I had to say mattered.

Consistently and then at a hastening pace, I began adding people to follow who espoused the goals and beliefs I wanted in my life. Fervently, I read my feed first thing in the morning, supplanting my newspaper reading in the morning. This was so much better. Since I followed all my favorite news outlets, I had access to every single piece of writing and then some. There was so much information out there, it could have been easy to be overwhelmed and turned off, but I ate it up like Pac-Man, and soon I was ready to do more than lurk.

"What is this Twitter thing you are always talking about? It's like Facebook right? Lots of status updates?" My colleagues jest with me all the time, now that I'm Twitter obsessed. I'm not the type to just dabble in anything; when I'm in, I'm all in, and I want to help others get it too. My PLN embraced me at the gate. It had been a while since I felt so excited about teaching. That reconnection was the rejuvenation my career needed, and my pedagogy is better for it.

It wasn't until I began participating in Twitter chats that I became exposed to a much larger community of educators who were connecting with their writing on a regular basis. I agreed with a lot of what I read, *and* I love to write, so I thought, "why not?" Soon 140 characters just weren't enough, and I felt a need to extend my ideas on the blog.

I was reluctant to just jump in for a while, but once I started, there was no stopping me. When someone posts a question, that you have an answer to, it's hard to stay silent. So the conversation begins. Developing relationships with strangers who become colleagues,

> Twitter was like my gateway drug to public writing.

then friends, is rewarding; they become the people who will cheer you on when you're ready to make a change. The educators on Twitter provided me with the boost of confidence needed to take the plunge, and I haven't looked back. It turns out that what I have to say does impact those who read it, and I'm not alone.

Blogging to Connect: Thoughts and Musings (A sample post from my blog)

The blank page sometimes beckons me.

A gentle "psst" in my ear, reminding of the necessity of thinking, reflecting and writing for the improvement of my craft, demanding I connect with myself and with you, my audience, also looking for the opportunity to nod your head in agreement or pause in question.

Writing, like teaching requires practice and revision sometimes done with a scalpel, other times with an ax. Either way, blogging offers the opportunity to determine which is needed and the time and regularity to fine tune the skills needed to work with both well.

Less than two years ago, blogging became a part of my everyday routine. Born out of the need to continue the reflecting process from the National Board [National Board Teaching Certification is where a teacher goes through a year-long reflective process that shows his or her effectiveness as a teacher. Being certified is the highest level of professional certification for teachers PreK–12] experience, I sat before the laptop and considered my pedagogy; not just the actual teaching, but the lifestyle of being an educator. As an educational blogger, there are many aspects of our lives worth thinking about and then adjusting to improve.

Many educators spend a good amount of time honing our skills, cutting our teeth and making essential mistakes so we can become better. Some of us are brave enough to honestly talk about the challenges and

(Continued)

(Continued)

successes—for both personal and collaborative reasons, but mostly in the name of growth.

It dawned on me last night while participating in #ntchat, a new teachers' chat, that I don't just blog to think about me, I blog to connect with others. Craving the feedback of my peers and a deeper relationship with people I've never met.

Here are some compelling reasons and benefits of blogging as a teacher:

- It forces me to look at what I'm doing all the time—writing a daily blog can be time consuming, but the reflective process is essential to becoming better. I can't just preach it to my students, I have to live it to show my students. Modeling is a huge part of writing and teaching, so why miss the opportunity here?

- As a writing teacher, I actively practice what I preach. I'm a writing teacher who writes. I helps me develop some credibility among my students and peers. While developing a personal brand, credibility associated with your name is everything.

- Honest accounts of what happens during my day, helps me connect and help others in similar or more challenging situations.

- Putting out the signal that help is needed, gets me lots of assistance when I need it. Actively asking for help is hard for me, but Twitter and my blog have made it easier. This confessional style of writing has made me a more vulnerable but empowered person and teacher.

- Becoming a part of a blogging community, makes me a reader and also offers more ideas to bring into the classroom to increase my students' new learning experiences.

- It helps my failures feel more like stepping stones—because I'm not just denying them, but recognizing and rectifying them.

- My blog records what goes on in my classroom and professional life, so it also serves as historical perspective—posterity.

Eagerly I share my stories, one to get them out and improve and two to hear back from my readers that they get it. The camaraderie and fervent innate understanding that can only come from other educators is part of what I longed for. I'm not too big to admit that.

Why do you blog or if you don't, what has been stopping you?

SO MAYBE YOU'RE NOT A WRITER

Blogs are more about authentic, honest voice; people read them to connect and learn with the writer. The writer writes them to engage with himself or herself and the authentic audience he or she is developing. This is crucial to understanding the necessity of blogging.

People have said it takes a village, and blogging is very much about the creation of a learning community. We share ideas, hoping for feedback, both positive and critical, depending on how it resonates with our readers.

Here are some tips to help develop your voice:

Honesty	Be honest, especially if you experience a perceived failure; while reflecting, try to see the positive takeaway from the experience and share both parts. The struggle can be a very powerful and motivating aspect to share.
Be detailed	Tell your stories, not anyone else's; people want to get to know you and connect with you. The best way for them to do this is for honest storytelling. Talk about what you know and what you want to know, *not* what you think people want to read.
Take risks	Take risks in format, in ideas, and in storytelling voices. They may not always work the way you want, but they will always yield progress. This behavior

(Continued)

(Continued)

	also needs to permeate what we present to students. As they get older, their ability to take risks comfortably in their learning decreases because they fear being wrong. This is a great opportunity to model that making mistakes is a good thing.
Develop a writing routine	For example, I read my Twitter feed each morning, try to read and respond to a few people's blogs, and then have a specific time set aside to try to write each day. Some days I write more and schedule posts ahead, and then other days I'm less productive. But every day, I write.
Read aloud	Read your posts aloud before hitting submit or scheduling in advance to ensure few, if any errors are made (I do make mistakes sometimes though . . . they slip through . . . largely because I skip this step in haste at times). Reading aloud also helps one hear the flow of the writing and feel the cadence, Ask yourself, "Does this make sense?" You can solicit this kind of feedback from your readers too.
Questions	End your posts with a question or an opened-ended call for your readers to engage. I'm always eager to hear what they have to say. Specifically inviting readers to respond by leaving a question is a great way to elicit feedback. We are all hardwired to answer questions when we see them.
Tirades and rants	Try to avoid going off on tirades or rants unless you can produce positive outcomes. No one wants to read straight-up negativity. Yes, this is *your* space, but do you want your space to be a soapbox? Writing of this kind does not encourage readers or rally them; it alienates them and yourself. Although we all need to let off steam from time to time, this may not be the right forum to do it in *unless* you are able to find the silver lining within the same post.
Back up your opinions	Back your opinions up with facts: always support ideas with experience or other materials and information to develop credibility. You want your readers to be able to trust you, so present honest representations of your work and experience. Be able to stand by anything you write. If you won't stand behind it, don't write it. Sensational writing may serve you in the short term but won't help develop credibility, which will ultimately lose you readers.

| Visuals | Try to have a visual with every post too, like pictures or infographics. They break the text and help with readability. Visuals don't have to be photos only. There are websites like ReciteThis and Quozio that will allow the user to create pull quote art that works nicely as a way into the writing. It's good to put the visual near the top of the post. If the post is long, visuals are a great way to break up the text midway through as well. Try not to chunk visuals in all in one place; this will defeat the purpose of using them. |

WHAT TEACHER HAS NOTHING TO SAY?

The number one reason many educators procrastinate when it comes to blogging is that they claim they have nothing to write about. We talked about voice a lot above and the necessity of being true to it, but what we haven't addressed is what to write about. The same way free choice is overwhelming to students at first, the sheer volume of topics to cover can render the writer paralyzed. It's ironic that folks who make a living out of content- and skill-related instruction, all of a sudden are short of tongue.

Trust me; you aren't at any loss for topics to write about. You probably just think that what you have to say isn't as valuable as it is. Each of us has a unique but similar experience of teaching. Individual to our learning spaces and personalities, like our teaching style, our voices sound differently to everyone, but the overall teaching life is one of commonality. Whether you write about specific classroom reflections or personal situations related to teaching, whatever you choose will be of use, not only to yourself and to your practice, but to your fellow colleagues.

So what should you write about? Here are a few suggestions, just to get your mind going:

The only thing really standing in your way is you. Brainstorm a list of topics that matter to you. The blog can address a niche, or if you don't want to pigeonhole yourself, it covers all things life. That is

Possible Blog Topics to Get You Started

- Why you decided to blog
- The first day of school
- Risks you plan to take and want others to hold you accountable for
- Goals—either short term or long term
- The work/life balance
- Standards-based reflection: either how you teach students to do it, or Danielson reflection based on observation feedback
- Failures that yielded growth
- How-to posts helping others to find the success you have found
- Personal stories of growth or challenge in the classroom
- Planning in all forms—how to plan, what to plan, reflection on plans made
- Content-specific lessons and modeled outcomes showing student work

Check out the Corwin Connected Educators website for more ideas.

your only choice and you are free to change your mind. Bear in mind that you are creating a brand with this blog, and at the very least it should represent you honestly and appropriately. Be mindful of the topics you choose and how you share them. Expletives may be fun in conversation, but if you have more descriptive language that won't make your blog unreadable for certain audiences, I recommend you go with that.

Students, colleagues, administrators, and other professionals may find time to read the blog; generate a brand you are proud to associate with. Understand that many folks will feel as if they know you through reading about your experiences, and the choices you make will either endear them to you or alienate them from you. Always adhere to an honest portrayal of yourself. Granted, none of us are one-dimensional, but modeling good choices is a huge part of taking the blogging leap. Once you go live, the world will be watching. What advice would you give your students?

NO TIME IN THE DAY FOR REFLECTION?

Teaching. Grading. Conferences. Parent communication. Planning and more unforeseen circumstances that you ever thought possible. When you're a teacher, there is *always* something to do, so when can we ever make time to write? If you haven't realized the urgency yet, then I'm not doing my job.

In education, blogging is like having a baby, there is actually no best time to start, you just have to jump in and start trying when the inclination hits. Only thinking about what we do isn't enough, we must set time aside to write about it, really reflect on the variety of challenges and successes we experience throughout each day. Keeping this record will help us improve and grow as educators.

One last thing to consider is how many posts you should write. Believe it or not, too much of a good thing really is too much. If you have lots to say once you get started, that's great, but rather than post it all on a day when you have great productivity, space it out. Most platforms have the ability to schedule posts for the future, and that is recommended.

> Routines are essential in education. Make blogging a part of your daily routine. If daily is too ambitious, start monthly and then upgrade to weekly. Once you see the benefits of blogging, it will compel you to keep up with it. Mind your media diet and allow yourself to really model the growth mindset.

People have different reading habits, and in order to get maximum exposure on each post, let a post linger for a day before you share new material. There will be exceptions as with everything, but certainly consider the saturation level of your content within your audience. Many people will unfollow or mute accounts on Twitter because of supersaturation in their feed. One post a day is a solid goal if you are the kind of person who writes regularly.

Blogging for Transparency and Resources

Transparency is essential for schools and for developing a brand that represents the appropriate message. Social media is out there for better or for worse now, so why not use it to your advantage to create the brand that is best for your school? Maintaining blogs for the district, administrators, teachers, and students can present the panoramic view of learning that goes on regularly in your space. Parents and community members can interact and participate in developing the school brand.

School leaders create spaces online in their blogs to share resources and information. If there is an upcoming school event that leaders want all stakeholders to get involved in, the blog can be a great place to promote the events or learning opportunities or both. Through the blogs and the social media links attached to them, it is easy to share information and get social involvement and feedback.

Another great aspect of blogging is the ability for school leaders to model appropriate digital citizenship for students. With the increasing amount of time that students spend online through social media, the need to show students positive brand promotion has increased. Kids need to understand that everything they post leaves a footprint and that how and what they are posting can leave a lasting impact on their lives. If we as education leaders actively act in the way we want kids to be acting, students will have a solid example of how best to show themselves to the world.

Blogging is a fortuitous chance that educational leaders must seize. Students may be accustomed to seeing teachers and administrators in school—in person, watching them conduct themselves in this way—but it isn't often that they experience us on the Internet or even in writing beyond the assignments we provide for them. Offering this additional dimension to who we are and what we think can only foster greater relationships with students and parents. Why shouldn't students see us the way we see ourselves, understanding the challenges and struggles we endure and overcome? The more students can connect with us as people, the more they will understand the ways we are the same and why paying close attention to our words matters.

Reasons Educators Blog

"As a teacher I blog as a way to connect what happens in my classroom to families, students, and all stakeholders. There are great learning achievements that happen every day in my classes and when I share the learning reaches beyond the wall of my room. With my subject area of music, I also blog to make connections to other subject areas to demonstrate multi-faceted, integrated learning and my blog is one place to showcase that."—*Jennifer Andrews, Elementary Music K–5 at Grafton Elementary School/Woodview Elementary* http://everythingconnectswithmusic.blogspot .com/

"I started as a way to organize and save my thoughts as I transitioned from the classroom to administration. Now I do it to share my voice, to get feedback, and to reflect."—*Brian Costello, Teacher at Weymouth Township School* www .btcostello05.wordpress.com www.creatingsuperheroes.word-press.com

"I found that the more you give, the more you get. I started blogging and commenting on blogs at about the same time. The more I commented, the more I wanted to write more blog posts, the more I wanted to comment, the more I wanted to blog, the more I . . . you get the idea.

I find that I always love to hear other people's ideas face-to-face. I knew that reading about other people's ideas could be even more fun!

Just as students learn more about mathematics by talking to one another about mathematics, we as teachers should take that same advice. The more we collaborate across the web, the more multi-faceted our lessons can be."—*excerpted from Megan Schmidt, HS Mathematics Teacher at St. Francis High School* http://mathybeagle.com

*See the appendix for a list of noteworthy educators who blog

REFLECTION QUESTIONS

1. What scares you about blogging?
2. What are you most passionate about? Can you put that passion into words?
3. What is one thing you'd like to accomplish with a blog?
4. What do you enjoy about those blogs?
5. What do you have to say to your audience?
6. What is one honest story or experience you'd like to share with readers?

Ready to Start, Now What?

SETTING THE STAGE FOR BLOGGING

Once you've decided to make the leap, there are a number of preliminary decisions that have to be made. The same way you would choose the style of notebook and pen you'd like to write with, you need to choose which platform is going to best suit your needs. Since you've already considered what you are hoping to accomplish with your blog, now it's time to select a platform that will work best to suit those needs.

WHAT ARE MY PLATFORM CHOICES?

Below is a list of some of the most popular blogging platforms to consider. Each has pros and cons depending on how you plan on using them. There are other platforms out there, but these are the most widely used in education. Once you select the one that best suits your needs, getting started will vary based on your choice. Most require an e-mail address and provide easy-to-follow setup instructions.

PLATFORM	PROS	CONS
Blogger™	• Affiliated with Google and can be linked to an existing Google account • Free mobile app available • Free • Easy to use with many free themes and looks • Privacy options available • Can add multiple authors to each blog • Can post blogs via e-mail • Automatically posts to Google+ for greater audience reach	• Limited in its ability to be adjusted or personalized. • Difficult to set up on your own domain • Poor customer service as it only comes in the form of user boards and YouTube videos
Edublog	• Affiliated with Wordpress but specifically for education • Allows for easy creation and management of student and teacher blogs • Mobile app availability • Can customize look of blog • Free and paid versions available • Been around a while, so very stable environment	• Ads on the site • No availability for automatic contributor links; they can be added to a blogroll, but this is time-consuming • Free version is extremely limited
Tumblr	• Free blogging platform • Free mobile app is available • Extremely simple to start and continue using—it can be a nice transition between Twitter and a blog before trying a more robust platform • Don't need to write anything, can just reblog other content • Known for its multimedia function	• Tends to get caught up in Internet blockage in schools • Not specifically geared toward education; therefore, other inappropriate content could show up on the site

PLATFORM	PROS	CONS
Weebly	• Free and paid versions available • Extremely easy drag-and-drop format for building websites with no tech background • Free mobile app available • Dynamic themes available across platforms • Privacy functions available • Ad free • Great referral program • Has an education platform with special features specifically for teachers • E-mail support, even for free accounts	• Few shortcuts on basics that would make the site more versatile • Free version is very limited for classroom use in terms of file size, uploads, and space. • No user management—users won't have profiles • Can't migrate information once used here as it won't copy and paste • No spam protection • No comment moderation • Can't modify certain aspects of layout
WordPress	• Free and paid versions available, both very effective depending on what you want to use it for. (Wordpress.com vs Wordpress.org) • Easily customizable, with many options to really control the look and feel of the site • Posting is simple and like using a word processor • Free mobile app available for paid sites • User registration and profiles available • Good e-mail support • Privacy functions and spam widgets available	• Can be overwhelming with the many options, and for the non-tech savvy, having too much of a good thing can be confusing. • Many of the additional functions will go unused • The free version doesn't offer mobile accessibility and is extremely limited in customization functions • Free version has ads

Now that you've seen your options, which one will it be? Which pros support what you need, and which cons won't hinder that effort? Get ready for a short setup and coming up with the perfect blog name. When naming your blog, consider searchability and branding. Do you want to use your name or something else? Make sure the URL you choose with the name, even for free sites, is simple. Sites with long URLs can get messed up and may hinder people from going to your blog. Every choice should be intentional.

VANITY URLS AND SELF-HOSTING

When you are ready to move from a free blogging site or you want to customize your URL (unique web address like www.starrsackstein.com), you can use a platform like Wordpress.org and buy hosting that provides you with a little more freedom and customization.

This is not mandatory, but it does help with branding and storage. You need to register your domain to assure that no one else has it and it is yours for the period of time you buy it for.

It will also help with sharing links to your site as free sites often have much longer URLs that will eat up your characters in social media networks like Twitter. Once you start getting into the habit of using URL shorteners to share more readily, it can negatively affect your search engine optimization or SEO (which is a long story for another time.).

There are many hosting choices for all kinds of money, starting as cheap as $10 a year. Depending on your needs and what you plan on using the site for, do a little research to see what price level and services provided work best for you. Choosing a host can be overwhelming, so ask around and see who others use. The most important questions to ask have to do with customer service. If something goes wrong with your site, you want to make sure you have access to the company in order to get things back to normal as quickly as possible. Here are some examples of hosting companies: Host Gator, Go Daddy, iPage, BlueHost, and many more.

 Visit our companion website for more consumer reports on the hosting options.

SETTING UP YOUR BLOG USING THE BLOGGER PROGRAM (EACH PLATFORM SETUP WILL VARY)

Step 1—If you are going to use the Blogger program, and you already have a Gmail account, it's as simple as going to the apps box in the upper right corner (it looks like a grid of boxes). Scroll down until you see the orange "B" icon and click to open the Blogger program.

FIGURE 2.1

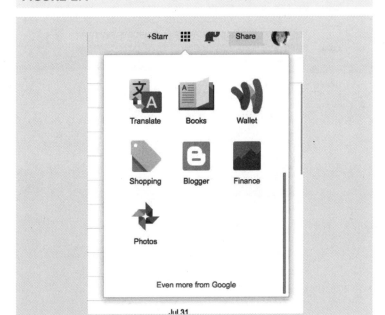

SOURCE: Google.com

If you don't have a Gmail account you can go straight to Blogger.com and start the process directly from their site, as you will not be able to access the apps grid from a different kind of e-mail. In order to use a Blogger account, you will have to create a free Gmail account before you can set up your blog. Follow the directions on the screen to do that.

Step 2—Once you open the Blogger program, you will need to complete a couple of steps before your blog is ready to go. First you will need to click on the "Create a new blog" button and the below screen will pop up. You will need to come up with an original title and an original address. The Blogger program will let you know if the address is available. It may take a few tries before you get one that isn't being used. So get creative but not too obscure.

FIGURE 2.2

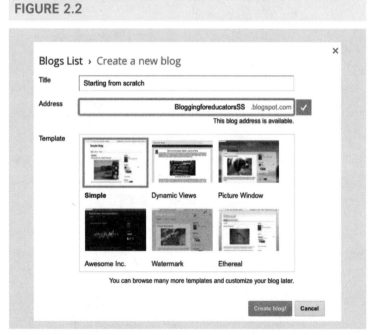

SOURCE: Blogger.com

Once you get the message that reads "This blog address is available" under the address line, it's time to select a template (or theme) for your blog. The Blogger program has a library to choose from. Browse the library until you find one you like. Don't worry if you end up changing your mind; the template can easily be changed later. All that's left for this step is to hit the orange "Create blog!" button in the lower right corner. Now you're in business.

Step 3—Figure 2.3 is a screenshot of the next page you will see after you click the "Create blog!" button. The Blogger program will take you directly into your first post. There are many things on this page, some that are essential to your getting a post published and others that you can worry about at a later time. In the next chapter, I will go into depth on some of the functions you see here, but for right now, let's just get a completed post under your belt.

FIGURE 2.3

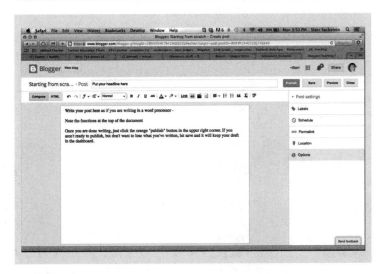

SOURCE: Blogger.com

Key elements to this page that you need to know are the following:

FIGURE 2.4

SOURCE: Blogger.com

- **Post** (top empty text box)—this the headline of your blog post. As you type in the headline, a unique URL will be created for that particular post based on the title.

FIGURE 2.5

SOURCE: Blogger.com

- **Compose**—this opens a blank document page as above. It looks like a Google or Word doc, which might be a plus for a school already using the Google Apps for Education system. You start typing the body of your text here. Stay in "compose mode" as you won't need to worry about code—the HTML version will put up text function and HTML code. You can learn this later or never if you don't want to. You don't need to know code to blog.

FIGURE 2.6

SOURCE: Blogger.com

- **Publish button**—in the upper right corner of the page, is the button you will press when it is time to make your post go live (ready for others to read).

- **Save button** (next to publish)—once you've started writing but you aren't ready to publish, you can save your draft until you feel you're done. Once you've saved your draft, you can find it here (see below). Your posts page will have a list of all your published posts as well as draft posts. The ones that haven't been published will have the word *draft* next to it in orange. You can return to the draft by clicking on the title. It will remain a draft until you click on "publish."

FIGURE 2.7

SOURCE: Blogger.com

- **Preview**—this will allow you to see what the post will look like live. Use it to see if the page looks and sounds as you want it to.

FIGURE 2.8

SOURCE: Blogger.com

- **Close**—this will shut the page. It will prompt you to either save the draft or abandon it.

REFLECTION QUESTIONS

1. How did you decide which platform was best for you?
2. What additional information do you need to feel confident starting your blog?
3. Have you visited the companion websites or viewed YouTube videos to supplement your questions?

Let's Get Technical, So You Can Hit Publish

S o you've set up your blog and now it is time to get a little more technical. All platforms will be a little different, but most share the below similarities with minor variations. As you generate the look and feel of your blog, consider your personality and what you want to communicate to your audience.

FIGURE 3.1

- **Site structure**—Most blogs have basic elements: a home-page, which is where readers land on your site, and additional pages that can be added through a dashboard where you will find all of the functions (see sample WordPress.org homepage in Figure 3.1). Additional pages worth including are an "about me" page where the author shares pertinent information about themselves to develop credibility (add work experience, school, or something personal), and different class pages that may be added if your site is being used expressly for school. Other examples of pages to include could be speaking engagements, publications, services, and the like.

FIGURE 3.2

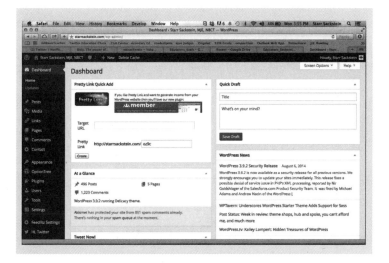

- **Dashboard or control panel**—This is home base. When you are editing your site, including but not limited to adding posts, you will be on your dashboard. The look of dashboards varies from platform to platform, but this will be the place for building and developing your blog. Figure 3.2 is a sample Wordpress dashboard. Figure 3.3 is a sample of a Blogger program dashboard. On the Blogger program's dashboard, Google provides help tutorials for new users. You can learn more about the functions of these parts on our companion website.

FIGURE 3.3

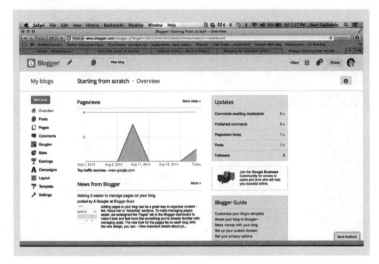

SOURCE: Blogger.com

- **Themes**—Most blogging platforms give options for the look of the blog by way of theme. The theme usually addresses the color scheme, layout, and look of the blog. When making the theme choices, consider readability and personality. Does the theme convey the message that your words will say? Make sure to have a congruent message. Also, consider responsive themes so that people who are reading your blog on different devices (screens of different sizes) have a good and easy reading experience. Responsive themes automatically adjust to the device they are being read on. Themes also are responsible for fonts, columns, and sidebars. Themes can be free or paid.

- **Basic posting**—This is relatively easy. It's like writing in a word processor and even looks like a Google or Word document with a fewer functions. You'll be able to spell check and use bullet points or numbers for lists, but you won't be able to use advanced functions like animation. Once you're done writing, you simply hit publish or submit (the button may be different depending on which platform you choose).

Make sure you stay in compose mode, as HTML mode will look different and require some knowledge of coding. There will also be less editing functions available as you will need to code to make it happen. In compose mode, the platform will automatically add the code accordingly.

FIGURE 3.4

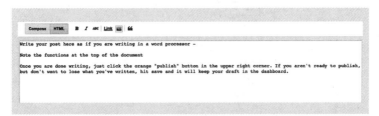

SOURCE: Blogger.com

- **Developing categories, keywords, labels or tags**—To help organize your blog and make it more searchable, you'll be able to "tag" your posts with specific keywords or phrases that will call up the posts in a search. You create tags in the tag section of the blog separating each word or phrase by a comma. Creating categories also automatically separates posts when you search for a particular category. This makes finding older posts easier and helps Google put you in their search as well.

FIGURE 3.5

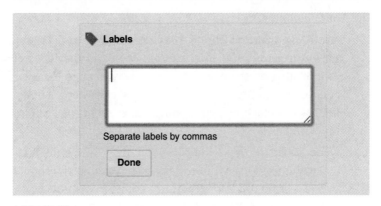

SOURCE: Blogger.com

- **Use of images**—Make sure that you only use images you take or borrow with permission. Using visuals in your posts is important; they are an additional entry point for readers and add interest in the writing. Try to always use captions with pictures and diagrams that add value to your post. Some platforms allow you to have a featured image as well as an in-post image. The featured image is the one that appears when you share the post.

- **Hyperlinks**—It's easy to add outside supplemental information by highlighting the text you want to hyperlink (above in the Blogger compose setting, it is shown as "Link." It is often depicted as an actual chain link.), clicking on the chain link icon at the top and then putting in the URL of the link you want to provide as support. This is a good way to link back to older posts in your blog that are relevant to the one you are writing now. It is also a good way to provide additional background information about ideas readers may need help with.

- **Using different fonts and other stylistic buttons**—Stick with a readable font that is a reasonable size. Younger kids will want to do more of a handwriting look, but sticking with clean and easy to read is best for everyone. Make sure it is also a color that is easy on the eyes. If a black or dark background is chosen, a white font is appropriate. If a light background is chosen, then black should be used. Be mindful as well that hyperlinks will come up as different colored text. To break up text, it is sometimes appropriate to use bold fonts or underlining.

- **Numbered and bulleted lists**—People love to read lists. They can get a lot of information across and they are not intimidating on the page. It's a great way to engage readers and easy to insert into a post. Be mindful of the length of the lists, as too much of a good thing can often get played out. More isn't always better.

- **Read more or more button**—You don't want a full 300–700 word post to be visible on the front page, so you should consider using the "More" button in order to keep the home page clean. A good rule of thumb is to keep the image and length of words on the page about equal, usually around 100 words to give the reader enough to be interested, but not everything, so they have to click to read the rest of the post. Some themes do this automatically, so it may be one less thing to worry about if you choose one of those.

- **The quote function**—This is another good way of breaking up text for readers. If you have a quote by someone else, or you have a piece of writing you want to stand out, highlight that bit of text and use the "" function. This will indent your quote and automatically italicize it to make it stand out more for the reader.

- **Mobile accessibility**—Having a platform that you can blog with from your phone is very useful. Students and teachers can do work while they travel and can also read blogs on the app that are specifically formatted for their particular device. Most platforms have mobile accessibility and students or teachers can save as a draft after they get their ideas down rather than publish from the phone. Inserting pictures is exceptionally easy using the mobile devices though.

Tips for Writing Engaging Posts

- Keep posts relatively short, 300–600 words, always remembering audience and readability. This isn't to say that longer posts don't work too, where appropriate. Vary what and how you are writing while staying true to your voice.

- Make sure the headline is catchy, but not necessarily misleading— using a verb to keep it active is helpful. Headlines are also important for search engine optimization (SEO)—when you use appropriate keywords, Google and other search engines will pick up your writing in a search about particular topics.

- Keep paragraphs short and use active words—make sure that sentences are varied and you aren't using the first person too often.

(Continued)

(Continued)

- You can use the second person (you) but be careful not to alienate your audience.

- Be mindful of tone with your words and structure.

- Avoid redundancy with word choices as this is a relatively short piece of writing.

- End with a question to engage readers and encourage them to interact.

- Make sure your image has an interesting caption that suits the picture and article, but doesn't repeat anything. A picture or a graphic is another entry point, so make sure to use it that way providing new and connected information that adds depth to your post.

- Multiple entry points helps keep the reader with you for the length of the article. An entry point is any way you get a reader to come in. The following are some examples: a headline, a lead (first sentence), a picture and caption, a pull quote, or a question.

REFLECTION QUESTIONS

1. Which platform would best suit your needs and why?
2. What challenges are you having with the platform you've chosen? Where can you go to ask for help?
3. What do you plan on addressing in your blog?
4. Who is your target audience?
5. How do you plan on engaging your readers?

Connecting With an Audience

L et's face it; it's not enough to just write. If it was, we would continue writing in journals for no one else's eyes but our own. And although that is a valid form of expression and useful to many people, blogging is about developing a voice to create new content to share with an audience. This means the way we write matters because we want to invite readers to participate and contribute to the content we have created.

However, the same way classroom conversation and questioning skills must be learned, there is a level of etiquette that comes with participating in feedback and discussion online. We are responsible as teachers to model, explain, and teach appropriate and meaningful ways to develop dialogue on blogs.

COMMENTING: WHY AND HOW WE SHOULD DO IT

Post a Comment

Enter your comment...

Comment as: Starr Sackstein ⇕   Sign out

Publish   Preview   ☐ Notify me

SOURCE: Blogger.com

Most writers crave the knowledge that an audience is reading their work even if they are nervous about what that audience thinks of it. For the amount of effort it takes to leave a short comment, readers can really make a blogger's day and benefit themselves; leaving feedback helps to develop relationships and rapport where reciprocity is encouraged and maintained. In short, commenting constructively is one way of being a good digital citizen.

Commenting is another way of providing feedback to writers; readers need to make it count by being specific and appropriate. The writer gets information about how to improve and better serve his or her readers and the reader's voice gets heard and potentially gets someone to read and interact with them too.

Like with all feedback, it is completely acceptable to agree or disagree with the writer, but it is important to be constructive while doing so. Although it is nice to hear something is "good," there is not much growth that will come from such a vague comment.

Here are some tips for commenting on blogs:

- Always be specific; for example, make reference to something specific the person wrote about—either quoting them directly or paraphrasing.

- Agree or disagree for a specific reason that doesn't merely reiterate something they have already stated. Add value with your comments.

- Ask the writer questions if something seems unclear, but do it in a probing and curious way, not an accusatory way.

- It's okay to praise or even be critical of what the author wrote, but always provide a reason why.

- Keep it short.

Here are some tips for what *not* to do:

- Don't tell the blogger his or her writing is bad. If you notice many errors, you may want to contact the writer privately rather than humiliate them publicly.

- Don't ever be disrespectful or mean just for the sake of being so.

- Don't be vague or too general—sometimes if you have nothing productive to say, you're better off not saying anything.

- Don't bully in any way. Make sure that all comments cannot be misconstrued or interpreted in a negative way. Choose your words wisely.

Bloggers should always respond to comments in a timely fashion. It's a good idea to acknowledge that you appreciate that the reader took the time to read and share his or her thoughts about what you wrote. Thank them for this time, and then address the comment by adding value to develop a dialogue with the commenter.

There will be times when a reader does post something overtly negative that isn't constructive. There are a few ways to handle this:

- The blogger can delete the comment.

- The blogger can acknowledge the writer without engaging in a dialogue about what has been said. You can still thank them for their time, with a statement like this: "Thank you for taking the time to read my blog. I appreciate your feedback."

- The blogger shouldn't go tit for tat with the commenter, as addressing whatever the overtly negative comment has been will most likely come off as defensive and will only inflame the issue more.

Comment moderation

Simply put, comment moderation is a privacy setting option for bloggers. It allows the blogger to determine which comments should be seen by the public and also forces a delay for when the comment will go live to the public. This is most appropriate for student blogs as those are the ones where stray comments that are potentially harmful could be made and a short delay can prevent trouble.

FIGURE 4.2

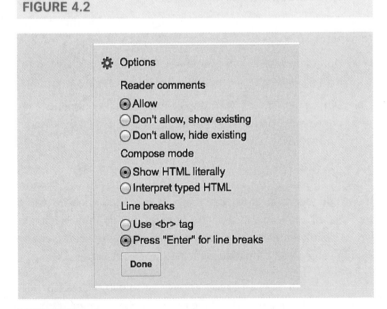

SOURCE: Blogger.com

For teachers and administrators, I wouldn't recommend using the moderation function. Bloggers should invite positive and negative feedback and by putting up an additional barrier to communication, it can turn readers off. Part of being able to read and comment on someone's blog is the immediacy of your comment's availability; it keeps the dialogue moving.

Even without comment moderation there are plug-ins a blogger can use to help with spam comments, which does happen from time to time. It's important to use a plug-in that will flag these kinds of "useless" spam comments and allow the author to delete on the back end rather than allow them to post. They don't automatically get deleted in case something else gets caught in the net that isn't spam.

In addition to comments, sometimes what you post will be reposted by another blogger and your site will receive a pingback. This allows you to know that your work is being shared in another place and the new blogger is giving you credit for it, providing more traffic directly to your blog. The pingbacks or trackback link will be listed at the bottom of your post in the comment area. On most platforms you can set it up to receive e-mails when new trackbacks are used.

PRIVACY MATTERS

Teachers and administrators who blog on nonprofessional content may fear the transparency and the ease in which the outside world can gain access to their work. Please remember that the main purpose one would write a blog is for this reason. Blocking out all outsiders works against what you are trying to do, which is building an audience. If what you are writing is that personal, be smart and keep it in a forum that is not meant for public consumption: a journal or a word doc under lock and key. This way, you will have no worries about the way you represent yourself or others' judgment on the sensitive information.

CREATING A COMMUNITY OF BLOGGERS

So now you have a blog. You're writing regularly. You're probably asking how we can turn this seemingly solitary experience into one that is collaborative and immersive.

It's all about creating a culture of reading and sharing. There are a few ways to share blog posts. Through the private blogs you can set up blogrolls (a list of blogs that can be followed by clicking on the link from the original blog). Through other platforms you can use the share buttons that most blogs come equipped with or use a plug-in that offers more options.

Some of the common social media sites worth sharing your work on are: Twitter, Facebook, LinkedIn and Google+. Each one will provide an opportunity to share with followers or target specific audiences depending on whom and how you decide to share.

Another blog sharing platform is Triberr which allows each user to start a tribe of his or her own or join an existing tribe based on the content of your blog. If you create a class Triberr, then everyone has the power of each other's audience built in. For example, I'm in a twenty-first century secondary education tribe. Others with like-themed topics ask to join and we attach our RSS feed to Triberr. Then as soon as we post a new article, it automatically is pulled into the tribe and each member of the tribe has the choice to share or hide the post.

Now, in a tribe where you don't know everyone, hiding a post would happen if the content doesn't match your personal brand. Part of what blogging allows you to do is create a personal brand that people come to know you by—it's how you will not only build your target audience, but also keep them coming back for more. So you don't want to share anything that contradicts or doesn't suit your audience. Your readers trust you and once you've developed a relationship with readers, you don't want to abuse it.

Widening your reach

Chat schedule down. Check. Share buttons attached to all social media. Check. Daily reading and commenting on other people's blogs, actively replying to those people who have been reading and commenting on your work. Check. Now what?

It's time to expand your reach. True success as a blogger within a community is when the writing appeals to more than just the people who know you or exist in your immediate circle of professional friends. The network you are developing must expand.

Good writing appeals to a wide audience of people. Aside from the education chats out there, content specific chats exist. Whether you're interested in politics, blogging, human resources, or leadership, there's something for everyone. You can begin to widen your reach by participating in these chats and sharing ideas and appropriate posts.

Another way to broaden your base readership is to use hashtags when sharing your work after you write. A hashtag widens your audience beyond just followers. Basically, it opens your exposure to a crowd specifically looking for information with that keyword. For example, I write a post about the struggles I experience balancing home and work and then I find a hashtag about parenting like #ptchat or #dadchat and I share my work there. Maybe I lurk on a few of these chats before I participate to get a feel for the audience. Once you feel comfortable, you can get involved. Remember, none of us are one-dimensional, our interests are varied, as is our knowledge base, so don't sell yourself short and only advertise to the known audience, expand.

Keywords are another way to reach a wider audience. If you tag your posts well, it will make them easier to find for search engines, and when eager readers are searching a particular topic, your post will be found. Making sure that your title has the right keywords also helps.

Is Connecting Everything When It Comes to Blogging? (A sample post)

Moments have passed since submit/publish has been struck and now the waiting begins. You've spent time, whether minutes, hours, or days crafting that post and although possibly insecure about the outcome, you went for it. After bolstering that courage to think, write, and share, it's time to hear what others say . . . or not.

It is easy to become obsessed with metrics and data about who is reading your work and what perception that provides you about it. Whether we are looking for connection, significance, or validation, as long as we are clear with ourselves about the learning, it doesn't really matter what other people think. There are many benefits to extending your reflection publicly as discussed throughout this book, but ultimately, your blogging experience is about you and your needs and the needs of your students. Look to fulfill those first, always, never seeking more than encouragement or dialogue from even the folks you admire most.

As a child, I was not the type to worry about what my peers thought of me. I was weird and I was okay with that. Marching to my own beat was kind of *my thing*, and with blogging it has been no different. That doesn't mean I haven't sat wondering why some posts appeal so widely to my readers and others that I have poured my soul into have not resonated as well. The moments of insecurity that begin to dwell and linger like pools of infested water after a storm, sitting and attracting disease-infested mosquitoes don't serve me well. So I acknowledge them and I let them pass, opting to focus more on the outcome of the reflection.

There was a period where I visited Teach 100 (a website you should consider submitting your blog to) every day to check my ranking among the world of educational bloggers. I'm not quite sure where the need arose from, but I noticed that I became too wrapped up in the number. So I stopped checking. It doesn't matter where I rank, if I'm getting what I need from the blog. And I am.

Although connecting is a big part of why we write publicly, it isn't the only thing. We blog to connect with ourselves and our experiences. So it's okay if you don't get a lot of readers at first (I know I didn't). It took a lot of effort of putting myself out there to attract people to my blog. I changed the theme, and restructured my personal time so that I could dial into the community consciously. It was an effort.

With that effort came pros and cons and it's important we remain cognizant of the time we spend connecting and at what expense. Our virtual personas shouldn't be the ones we connect most with, but rather an extension of the human us that the ideas represent. It's easy to start losing track of time once you get involved with Twitter and blogging, but moderation is key. These powerful tools are here to facilitate our growth as professional educators, but not with the trade off of letting our actual lives become less important.

As you push forward in this journey of connection, always remember balance. It's okay to take time off when you need it and it is also okay to escape to it in challenging moments seeking answers or space. The best advice is just be aware and never let yourself get too involved at the demise of something else.

What are some pieces of advice you would share about how you balance work and life?

REFLECTION QUESTIONS

1. What fears do you have about sharing your work with readers? What do you stand to gain by taking the risk?
2. How might you use commenting to teach digital citizenship while giving feedback?
3. What privacy concerns do you have for your or your students' blogs?
4. Why do you want to develop a community of writers in your class and how do you plan on starting?

Final Thoughts and Takeaways

B logging is an easy way to work on school promotion without the need of a PR person. The more members of a school community blogging, including administrators, teachers, and students, the better the picture the world has of the school. Each voice, each experience offers insight into the learning happening in all the spaces. Principals can communicate with the school and parents. Teachers can communicate with other teachers, colleagues, students, and parents; students can have an international audience to share their ideas and learning with. The conversation doesn't have to end in the four walls of the classroom.

Developing diverse ideas and being able to communicate them in writing is an essential tool in the twenty-first century. Each of us needs to be a vital member of the digital universe. As bloggers, we are naturally connected educators, sharing our ideas, collaborating, and modeling progressive and authentic behaviors for children growing up in today's landscape. Students become global participants and digital citizens prepared for success in their futures.

But blogging is really only the beginning. As connected human beings, we grow with our reflection, and as we share, we build relationships and make action. Blogging has the capacity to make the world smaller and offer tremendous resources everywhere. The more we develop our content, share our stories, and develop our voices, the more we build upon our own knowledge bases stretching it beyond what we know. This foundation of growth will be the building block of tomorrow's change, not only in education but also in society.

Once you get a handle on developing your brand, it's time to start thinking about expansion. Other avenues worth exploring are search engine optimization (SEO) and social media marketing to maximize audience and reach the targets necessary to move forward. Gathering that critical mass and now not only creating content, but using it to enact change in a positive way is essential. The highest goal must always be continued growth.

Another avenue to pursue potentially could be writing a book. I've used my blog to gain access and reflect, write, develop an audience, and learn what my readers want. Once you know and feel confident in your niche, whatever it is, it will be time to extend your writing experience and expand into a particular topic. Writing is limitless and full of opportunities; the blogging is just a step in a bigger picture.

So where will all of this connecting lead you? That remains to be seen. But it's time to take that first step. Connect with someone whom you admire. Watch them for a while. Read who they read and make note of similarities and differences. What resonates for you? Which voices make an impact? Where does your voice fit in the global conversation? As you begin to hone your own voice, allow it to be heard. Share it with your students and be their model as their journeys take shape. Encourage reading and writing on all levels and when you notice it making a change in each of your students' lives, tell them.

We are all better together. Growing, making mistakes, learning from those mistakes, and transparently becoming the best communicators we can be. This is how we will shift current paradigms and begin to enact change in the day-to-day experiences of all learners.

So it's time, are you ready? I challenge you to take a risk and go blog!

Appendix

Sample Elementary Educator Blogs

- Pernille Ripp's Blogging Through the Fourth Dimension—http://pernillesripp.com
- Erin Klein's Kleinspiration—http://www.kleinspiration.com/p/meet-erin-klein.html
- Colby Sharp's Sharpread—http://mrcolbysharp.com
- Craig Yen's Yen4Teaching—http://yen4teaching.blogspot.com

Sample Secondary Educator Blogs

- Dawn Casey-Rowe's Casey's Cafe—http://cafecasey.com
- Luann Lee—http://www.chemistar.com/blog/
- Chris Lehmann's Practical Theory: A View from the Schoolhouse—http://practicaltheory.org/blog/
- Starr Sackstein—http://StarrSackstein.com
- Amy Smith's Ramblings from a Middle School Teacher—http://ramblingsfromamiddleschoolteacher.blogspot.com

Sample Administrator Blogs

- Spike Cook—http://drspikecook.com
- George Couros's The Principal of Change—http://georgecouros.ca/blog/
- Brad Currie—http://www.bradcurrie.net
- Vicki Day's Rethinking Education—http://victorialday.wordpress.com
- Jon Harper's Bailey & Derek's Daddy—http://jonharper70.wordpress.com
- Joe Sanfelippo—http://www.jsanfelippo.com

- Eric Sheninger—http://ericsheninger.com
- Tony Sinanis's Leading Motivated Leaders—http://leading motivatedlearners.blogspot.com

Sample General Education Blogs

- Mark Barnes's Brilliant or Insane—http://www.brilliant-insane .com
- Vicki Davis's Cool Cat Teacher—http://www.coolcatteacher .com
- Peter DeWitt's Finding Common Ground on Education Week—http://blogs.edweek.org/edweek/finding_common_ ground/
- Starr Sackstein's Work in Progress on Education Week Teacher— http://blogs.edweek.org/teachers/work_in_progress/

A SAGE Company

Corwin is committed to improving education for all learners by publishing books and other professional development resources for those serving the field of PreK–12 education. By providing practical, hands-on materials, Corwin continues to carry out the promise of its motto: **"Helping Educators Do Their Work Better."**